CASHOLOGY

THE SCIENCE OF HOW TO LIVE A CASH ONLY LIFE

Put Your Financial Mind To Work

Hasheem Francis & Deborah Francis

For information about reprints rights, translation, or bulk purchases, please contact Deborah Francis at **info@BTPPublish.com** or you can write to Loyal Leadership Inc., and P.O Box 552, Plymouth, FL 32768   www.BTPPublish.com

CASHOLOGY The Science of How To Live A CASH ONLY Life
Authors: Hasheem Francis & Deborah Francis.
Cover design by: BTP Marketing Group
Edited By: BTP Marketing Group
ISBN: 0615647472
Published by: BTP Publishing Plymouth, FL (www.BTPPublish.com)

DISCLAIMER: This book was written for informational purposes only. This book is not to replace the financial advice of a qualified professional, who has demonstrated sound financial understanding in their life. If professional advice is needed, seek proper counsel.

Also by Hasheem Francis & Deborah Francis:

Built To Prosper

Built To Prosper For Women

Built To Prosper Financially

Built To Prosper Women of Wisdom Journal

Built To Prosper Wealth of Wisdom Journal

The Joy of Healthy Living; The Guide To Eating Right For Life

Cashology Academy Wealth Work

Cashology Academy Wealth Journal

Undeniable Confidence

The Science of Getting Rich: The Key To Peace, Power, & Prosperity

Seminars by Hasheem Francis & Deborah Francis

Built To Prosper For Life Seminars

Cashology Academy

The Joy of Healthy Living

Loyal Leaders Conference

Young Entrepreneurs Academy

Built To Prosper University

BTP Emerging Business BootCamp

CA$H OLOGY
ACADEMY

Cashology Academy Mission: *is to change the money chaser into a money master through wealth building and economic wellness.*

Cashology Academy is a leader in financial education, providing wealth-building education to empower individuals to live a CASH ONLY life.

Cashology Academy's goal is to help people achieve their maximum income earning potential by learning essential techniques to accumulating wealth.

Cashology Academy combines a team of trainers, mentors and coaches who possess practical, hands-on experience in their areas of expertise with a rigorous instructional design methodology and proprietary content-rich advanced courses to create rewarding client experiences.

www.CashologyAcademy.com

Dedications

This book is dedicated to all who have the burning desire to study and apply the Cashology principles and pass this wisdom on from one generation to the next.

- Hasheem Francis and Deborah Francis

Disclaimer

The information contained in this material is for information purposes only.

Cashology Academy does not hold itself out as providing any legal, financial or other advice. Cashology Academy also does not make any recommendation or endorsement as to any investment, advisor or other service or product or to any material submitted by third parties or linked to this material. In addition, Cashology Academy does not offer any advice regarding the nature, potential value or suitability of any particular investment, security or investment strategy.

The product and services mentioned in this book may not be suitable for you. If you have any doubts you should contact an independent financial advisor. In particular some of the investments mentioned may not be regulated under the Financial Services Act 1986 or at all and the protection provided to you under this Act will not apply.

We make financial suggestions and it is up to you to make your own decisions, or to consult with a registered investment advisor when evaluating the information of Cashology Academy.

CONTENTS

"If someone makes you feel like they are pushing you beyond your own limitations that is when you are in the presence of greatness. I know this from experience; my mentor does this to me every day."

- *Hasheem Francis*

"People don't change when they feel good. They change when they're fed up. Pain pushes us to those crucial turning points. And, one day, enough will be enough! The question is, are YOU ready for a financial change?" **Cashologist**

INTRODUCTION

We would like to commend you for your commitment to investing in your financial education. **Our mission is for One Million Families to become an example to their community of how powerful it is to live by CASH ONLY**. No matter the current condition of your finances, this book will assist you in creating a CASH ONLY mindset and wealth building lifestyle with a greater sense of ease and purpose. You can dispel any beliefs that you may have about being a financial victim. Throughout this book, we will share strategies that will help you create new beliefs that will put you in a position of financial empowerment.

"You may have a fresh start financially at any moment YOU choose. Financial "failure" is not falling down, but staying down. Dust yourself off and get back in the financial game."

A CASH ONLY life is powerful -- powerful enough to change the world for the good. Many people have asked us; "What is the meaning of CASH ONLY?" CASH ONLY is a mindset and a lifestyle. What we mean by CASH ONLY is that we as a community will live to build wealth and not be consumed by debt. The first important rule is to take responsibility for everything that happens in our financial life. We have decided to take control of our financial habits and take charge of our destiny. We understand that in order for things to change we must change.

1

The Principles in Living A CASH ONLY Lifestyle

Everything starts with change! People may want to change but often lack the tools to establish new financial habits. Most people maintain their current financial habits because it's simpler and less complicated than changing. Just deciding to change isn't enough. Your brain wants to cling to ingrained habits. It likes to repeat things that already work. It doesn't like learning new behaviors, because that takes energy and effort.

In order to reprogram your mind to accept higher levels of wealth, you must discover what beliefs have limited your experience in the past, and you must consciously decide to change those beliefs. If you do not realize it already, by the end of this book, it should be clear: YOU are the product of your own thoughts.

What you believe yourself to be, you are. It is not your intelligence, your education or your circumstances that have left you financially unsatisfied, but your limiting beliefs about what it means to be wealthy. **Do YOU believe you deserve to be wealthy?** So, why aren't you wealthy? Most of us have a subconscious idea of what we think we deserve. And when life does not represent what we think it should be like, we experience frustration and discontent, which can spur us into action to make change.

The moment you accept the responsibility for what's going on in your life, you will have found the power to change. It's important to figure out how money functions in your life. If you are serious about building wealth, you will have to learn how the wealthy think.

Our desire is for you to achieve the results in living a CASH ONLY lifestyle. This is serious business, so take your time in understanding and applying the principles in this book.

It is not good enough to just have hopes and desires to succeed; you must meticulously plan your financial goals and work at them until they become reality. Unbending belief and faith are the essential elements of bringing your vision of living a financially free life into physical reality.

I strongly believe that those who do end up succeeding financially are the ones who say they will, and back their words up with action. That is quite a bold statement to make, right? Well, I stand firmly by my words. I believe that the people, who say they can, often do. **Your attitude matters!** The higher your level of confidence, and your willingness to back that confidence up with action, puts you in the position to succeed.

It does not matter what kinds of things you have done in the past with your finances. The only thing that matters is what you are doing now. The only thing that will define you as a person is how you are living your life NOW. The past is the past; it is time to develop a cash only mindset.

All things are possible for you, especially when you have the right mindset and you are committed to achieving your financial goals. An improvement in your life begins with an improvement in your habits.

This book has been written because far too many people have allowed debt to overtake their life. Debt which you are unable to pay, back puts you in bondage physically, spiritually and financially. Obviously the greater the debt, the greater the bondage. **This is a very expensive price to pay for debt.** At the end of the day, we have to understand what we're doing with our money and be responsible for making better choices.

Change requires courage; not everyone is willing to do what is necessary to step outside of their comfort zone. Breaking old beliefs and habits is dependent upon you noticing them as the barriers to your financial success. You have power to control your thought processes, which have a profound effect on outcomes. If you think you can achieve something, it's more likely that you will.

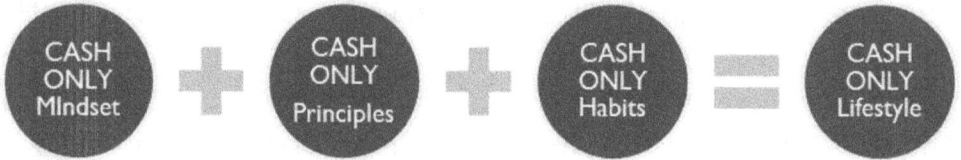

CASH ONLY MIndset **+** CASH ONLY Principles **+** CASH ONLY Habits **=** CASH ONLY Lifestyle

Condition Your Mind for Financial Success

Your mind is the key to your financial success. A right mental attitude towards money takes effort, patience and discipline. If you think someone is wealthy because they have money, you would be wrong. Having money is the effect, not the cause of their wealth. They have money because they THINK about money in a way that make them wealthy. The difference between those who are rich and those who are broke is in the way they think about money.

Once you're able to observe your own thinking, and recognize the difference between wealthy and broke, you grab hold of the power of choice. You must feed your mind with positive, nourishing thoughts about money. If you have a negative attitude toward those who are financially free or wealthy, do not expect to join the community of wealth builders.

A negative attitude towards money will keep you broke. Reprogram your mind with faith, hope and expectancy that you will join the elite club of those who live a debt free life.

"The only way to be wealthy is to know the rules in the financial game and USE them to the best of your ability." - **Cashologist**

The principles in **CASHOLOGY** are not new; you have heard most these principles before. What is unique about this book is that the information is put together in a way that is understandable and applicable to anyone. We all must deal with money while we are here on this earth. If you desire fresh food, clean water, a nice home, reliable automobile, gas, central air, or any amenity that adds comfort to your life, it requires money. M-O-N-E-Y.

This book will present viewpoints which all are related to using "**CASH ONLY**" strategies. It does not matter how much debt you are in at this moment, it can get better if you "decide" to change your attitude about money, learn how to manage your finances, and make a commitment to build wealth. **CASH ONLY is a money mindset, which creates a lifestyle.**

Make this book your daily companion. Condition your mind for success by applying the principles in this book. If you apply them consistently you will get measurable results. This is serious business; this is your life, so be committed to getting the results.

We have used the principles in this book to achieve more than we ever dreamed, imagined or desired. We have found what is truly important in life and we are still in awe of the unlimited possibilities that lie ahead. This is not just for us or a select few; we just stayed committed and got the results. And the same is going to happen for YOU, if you're willing to do what it necessary. Our desire is for you to develop a financial consciousness that would lead you to wealth. You deserve to be wealthy.

CHAPTER I:
DEVOLOPING THE CASH ONLY MINDSET

Your mindset and financial habits literally creates your financial life. Wealth is available to those who understand the principles and work for it. If you believe wealth is your birthright, then you are more than likely to create wealth. If you believe that money is scarce and hard to get, then that reality will manifest itself in your life. When you accept limiting beliefs about money, those beliefs gain control over your life.

The world is divided between people who are open to learning and those who are closed to it, and this trait affects everything from your worldview to your relationship with money. The truth about money is that everyone needs it; it's just that most people are too lazy to learn what it means to be wealthy.

The only thing that can hold you back is yourself and your own money myths. You succeed – or fail – according to the quality and content of your thinking. The type of goal you put in your mind determines the sort of action steps you develop. Your greatest asset or liability is your mind and how you use it. No mind ever receives the truth until it is prepared to receive it.

A mind that is not properly prepared for finances is a terrible thing to waste. The best possible investment you can make is in your financial education. Financial literacy is a language people must learn, yet knowledge about money is still a foreign concept for too many people. You are considered fortunate if you grew up in a household where your parents had positive open conversations about money. But for those who did not, your investment in your financial education is of the upmost importance.

You developed your financial belief system during childhood. It is a compilation of your experiences and the messages you received from your family, friends, and teachers and from everything you read or watched. Some of your beliefs work to your advantage, but it is the "erroneous" beliefs that hold you back from succeeding.

If you don't know who YOU are and what you value, nothing you do with your money will ever feel right. You can learn a lot about yourself through how you make, spend, save, and share your money. Your beliefs and habits shape your reality and influence your bank account.

"Many people completely fail in life or are forced to live in mortifying poverty, to struggle along perhaps under the curse of debt, miserable and handicapped all their lives because they never learned finance for themselves." **Orison Swett Marden**

THOUGHTS

BELIEFS
Money Experience

FEELINGS

What is Money?

Money is commonly defined as a medium of exchange. Someone once said to me, "Money is not everything." My reply was, "Go tell your mortgage and credit-card company that." Money brings power to the user. Money has no power in itself, but having control over how it will be used gives you power. Money is used to build beautiful cities, powerful armies, help oppressed nations; feed the hungry, and build a thriving economy. On the other hand, money can be used to exploit people and make them do things they normally would not do that are outside their moral teaching. The best way to acquire money is to EARN IT!

Your beliefs about money play a role in how much you earn. Many people feel powerless over their finances, and mistakenly think that if they just had more money, they would be more empowered. Money does not determine personal worth. Only YOU can do that. Money is meant to be used with a strong sense of discernment and wisdom. In order to handle large amounts of money, you must be mentally prepared to be a steward of it. **Money will control you if you do not have the right mindset for it**.

Studies show that no more than five people out of a hundred who have made money, know what to do with it and are able to hold on to it. If you need further proof, research those who have won the lottery. Most of the winners end up worse than before they gained their winnings. Why? They were not mentally prepared for the riches they received. They gained a large amount of money but they had the wrong money mindset, (easy come, easy go). They never developed the proper philosophy of saving and investing their money, they had the hand to mouth mentality.

Who is in Control of Your Money Mindset?

The number one stumbling block to reaching financial success for most people is that they do not genuinely believe that they deserve it. Who sold them on that story? Too many people let opportunities pass them by because their fear paralyzes them. Fear of success, fear of failure and inferiority complexes can all affect the way you feel about yourself and thus influence your ability to succeed. Learn to feel deserving of all life has to offer by loving and nurturing yourself. If you think in negative terms you will get negative results. If you think in positive terms you will achieve positive results. Negative thoughts create a negative atmosphere that can trigger an unwanted outcome. **YOU have the power, YOU are in control of your thoughts!**

Many people are motivated by money. It is not wrong to be money motivated as long as you are not controlled by money. Accumulating wealth in order to help others and earning money for the advantages it can offer you and your family are worthwhile objectives. Having enough money can liberate you from a stressful job, free you to follow your dreams and allow you to take care of your loved ones.

When all of your expenses are covered and you are relieved of the worry that comes with paying your debts, you can devote all your time and energy to the things that really matter to you in life.

There is a peace of mind that comes with financial stability. It allows you to set your own agenda for your life. Financial stability eliminates many of the "what ifs" associated with money worries. The more money you have, the more choices you have. Yes, you can be a wealthy! (I believe in YOU!)

Who had the greatest influence on your understanding about wealth?

Getting ahead requires the right attitude: the "Wealth Builder's Mindset." It also calls for careful planning. If you want to change the effect, you have to change the cause; your thoughts are the ultimate cause. With the right mindset, you can overcome any financial obstacle. Everyone has experienced a financial setback; how you handle them makes all the difference. When life deals you an unfavorable financial hand, don't sulk or complain. Act quickly to make things better. Don't let obstacles interfere with you getting ahead financially.

Never quit when the going gets tough. Instead, use bad events as learning experiences. Never stop growing because life will never stop teaching. People sabotage themselves financially when they are conflicted about their goals or feel unworthy of success. *You get what you believe you deserve. No more, no less*. When you face your fears and make the commitment to change, you can stop sabotaging your hopes and dreams. By changing your ingrained reactions and beliefs, you can achieve new, positive results. Each financial challenge you overcome it makes you stronger.

Your Internal Dialogue about Money

What stories do you tell yourself about your money? That you must work extra hard to earn it? That you have no time to create a financial plan? That being wealthy is an impossible dream? If this is your internal dialogue, then you should not be surprised if it is also your external reality. People constantly engage in ongoing dialogues with themselves, mostly on an unconscious level.

Your financial positive and negative self-talk affects how you feel. Your unconscious mind does not distinguish between "fact or fiction," so if you are repeatedly telling yourself negative statements, your unconscious mind will eventually believe them – even if they are untrue. If you tell yourself that you are a financial loser (your story), your mind will accept it as fact. The mind does not discriminate against the information that you fill it with. It will do everything possible to help you fulfill your negative or postive story. If your story is one of constant triumph over tough odds, you will almost surely overcome any and all financial obstacles.

Here are some ways you can begin using positive self-talk about money to develop a wealth builder's mindset. The first step towards creating positive money self-talk is to become more aware of how you speak to yourself about money on a daily basis.

The following strategies can help you become more conscious of your personal money self-talk blueprint.

1. Carry a note pad with you throughout the day and jot down your thoughts about money when you think of them.

2. Write a bulleted account of your thoughts on money throughout the day and a general description as to the experience that led to the thought and the experience that came after the thought on money.

3. At the end of the day, go back and reflect on the words that were chosen while speaking to yourself about money and how you can add positive language to describe money which will lead to more positive experiences in regards to the use of money.

Your new wealth building internal dialogue will become real the more you focus on it. This means "full commitment" in everything you do.

Success in wealth building requires intense commitment, engagement and focus. It means total dedication to the present, not to some vague future.

When you hear yourself saying something negative about money, just say "delete" or "I rebuke that" Just as if you typed an error on your computer and you hit delete to erase the error, do the same with a negative statement that may come out of your mouth. We were taught this strategy by a very successful entrepreneur from Montana and it has worked for us ever since.

As you notice yourself saying something positive in your mind about money, you can continue your thought and be able to reflect on it positively by smiling and saying to yourself, "I Am the Master of Money." Saying this aloud with feeling will be more powerful, and having to say it aloud will make you aware of how many times you are infusing positive self-talk thoughts. The truth about money is that if you have enough of it, you hardly think about it; but if you lack it, you will think of nothing else.

Never say that you can't do something, or that something seems impossible. We are limited only by what we allow ourselves to be limited by: our own minds.

We are the masters of our own reality; when we become self-aware to this: absolutely anything in the world is possible. As with any new habit, you need to work hard to embed your new wealth building internal dialogue into your consciousness. Self-affirmations like: "I am a wealth builder" or "I attract only lucrative, enjoyable and beneficial opportunities" are particularly empowering because they increase your sense of peace about money in any given situation, and they give you the ability to search for solutions. Open your consciousness about wealth which will make you more hopeful and will release your imagination to new possibilities.

The Ten Causes of Financial Failure:

1. Lack of Financial Literacy. Financial knowledge includes understanding how a checking, savings, and investment accounts works, knowing the difference between earned, passive, and portfolio income. Knowing how to read and put together a financial statement. The understanding of finances impacts the daily decisions an average family makes when trying to balance a budget, buy a home, fund their children's education and ensure an income for retirement.

Many people do not take the time to invest in their financial education. Research studies across countries on financial literacy have shown that most individuals (including entrepreneurs) do not understand the concept of compound interest, and some consumers do not actively seek out financial information before making financial decisions. 40% of working class adults would grade themselves a C or below for their knowledge of personal finance. Most consumers lack the ability to manage a credit card efficiently, and their lack of financial education is responsible for their lack of money management skills and financial planning. Your level of financial literacy affects your quality of life significantly. It affects your ability to provide for yourself and your family, as well as your contribution to your community. Financial literacy enables people to understand what is needed to achieve a lifestyle that is financially balanced, sustainable, ethical and responsible. Your financial success is in YOUR HANDS!

2. A Negative Attitude Toward Money. One may believe that having plenty of money is wrong due to the misinterpretation of the scripture: "For the love of money is the root of all evil." 1 Timothy 6:10 It is difficult to earn money if there is a negative attitude about it or if you have erroneous beliefs about wealth. You cannot attract something that deep in your heart you despise. This is a most common attitude for many people. They desire money but their attitude is negative and therefore, repellent.

If you want to attract money, you first have to get rid of all negative thoughts and attitude about it. With a negative attitude toward money, you will believe it is bad to have it and might even make some errors of judgment that would cause you to lose money. You would basically find a way to sabotage yourself financially. On the other hand, if your attitude is positive and you are open and willing to have wealth in your life, you will attract money through various income producing opportunities.

3. Lack of Self-Discipline with Money. The most difficult thing for most people is controlling their spending. If you cannot control your spending, then no matter how much money you make, it will never be enough. The lack of discipline in finances usually leads to debt, which is the #1 cause of stress. Without discipline, you will never be able to build wealth or join the financial elite. Discipline is being able to say no to impulse purchases. It is being able to do the things you do not want to do when you know you must. It is forcing yourself to do the things that are necessary to secure your financial future. The only way to keep from going backwards is to keep going forward. Discipline is the price of success. There are three steps and each one is absolutely essential: You must first have the knowledge of your power; second, the courage to dare; and third, the faith to do.

4. Trying to Keep up with The Joneses. Many people live beyond their means because they cannot bear to have other people think that they cannot afford certain luxury items. It used to be that spending money on status symbols for the sake of flaunting your wealth was an activity reserved for those who had the money to flaunt their wealth. That has all changed. For many, "keeping up with the Joneses" became an overwhelming obsession that led to financial ruin. What they buy and what they have is tangled up in their identity. Overspending is usually a psychological problem that manifests itself as a money problem.

People buy things that they think they should have because culture says that they are important (a certain make and model automobile, designer clothes, etc.).

Key strategy: Before you make a purchase, ask yourself: "Am I really using this money in a way that is going to be a benefit to my financial future?" Is this an asset or liability? I hope you know the difference. Be willing to make sacrifices when it benefits the bigger goal: financial freedom.

5. Lack of Vision for Financial Future. A person with no clear goal on what they want to accomplish financially is headed towards financial disaster. You cannot expect to have a vision for your relationships, your health and your spiritual life, yet neglect your finances. Money is important, no matter what others may say or what you may believe. To operate in this world, you are going to need money so why not have a plan for it? Your goals are not the same as anyone else's and they do not have to be. The key is identifying what you want, setting priorities and making a plan. When you get clarity in your vision, it gives you energy. When people get a grip on what they are going to accomplish and where they are headed, it sweeps away many mental roadblocks to action.

6. Comfortable with Being an Underearner. Do you earn less than your potential despite your need or desire to do otherwise? If so, you may be an underearner and all the budgeting in the world may not help you until you address the underlying issues that are holding you back. Those who are comfortable with being an underearner lack the ambition to move past mediocrity. Many people complain about not earning enough income on their jobs, but they are not willing to do what it takes to earn more. Why accept a job that is not paying you what you are worth?

You cannot blame the job; you are the one who accepted the position. If you want to earn more, be more and do more, so you can have more. Are YOU willing to invest in yourself, to develop the skills needed to be a wealth builder?

7. Selfish with Money. A person who has no desire to share with those less fortunate will not achieve high levels of prosperity. They see giving money to those in need as a loss and less as a duty. The more we give, the more we shall get; we must become a channel whereby wealth can flow through.

I am not saying to go out and just give your money away. You must use wisdom when giving money; there will be many people who will try to take advantage of your kindness and then there are those who just want to keep their hand in your pocket. Those who are selfish only look out for themselves. You will find that broke people are more selfish with money than wealthy people. Broke people see giving money to charity as a financial loss or they make the excuse that they have nothing to give. Wealthy people see giving as an obligation; they look for ways to spread their wealth where it can be of greatest service to mankind.

8. Forget Who Is the True Source of Wealth. "If you start thinking to yourselves, "I did all this. All by myself. I'm rich. It's all mine!"—well, think again. Remember that God, your God, "gave you the power to produce wealth." Deuteronomy 8:18

What does the phrase "power to produce wealth" mean to you? Many people put money before their health, family and spiritual beliefs. God is not bankrupt and we who are the representatives of God's power should not be bankrupt either. Our relationship to money is then a reflection of our relationship to God.

The source of my wealth is God. It is sometimes easy to forget that God is the source of all things, including our money and possessions. When I go to the bank, cash a check or receive any form of value as an increase in my wealth, I look to God as my source.

Look within to the true source of your wealth. Look for things in your life that represent abundance, health, wealth, happiness, and all the blessings that are already present.

9. Fails to Take Responsibility for Financial Circumstances. Have you ever met someone who blames any and everybody for their financial problems? I know someone like that, and he has a great deal of money.

I am struck, every time we meet, by his failure to take responsibility for what is happening in his financial life. Everything is someone else's fault. Every problem is explained away with reasons about why he cannot affect the situation or the outcome. If we deny our mistakes or fail to take responsibility for our finances, we fail to learn and improve. People who take complete responsibility for their finances experience joy and control of their money. They are able to make choices because they understand that they are responsible for their choices.

The most important aspect of taking responsibility for your money is to acknowledge that managing your finances is your responsibility. No one can be financially smart for you; people have their own issues with money they need to work out and they cannot take on your responsibility. You are in charge. Many have lost touch and disregarded the basic financial principles – to spend less than you earn and invest wisely for great returns. No matter how hard you try to blame others for the financial events of your life, each event is the result of the choices you made and are making.

10. Borrows Money with No Plans or Means to Pay it Back.

Borrowing money and not paying it back can and will ruin your reputation. When someone has to call a person a hundred times to get the money back that they lent, it can put a strain on the relationship.

I have lent money to friends and family members and borrowed money from friends and family members, and neither situation worked out well. I learned a lot from both experiences. Most importantly, I learned that I will never loan money to friends or family members again; I would rather have them work for it. I have loaned money to a family member and when they did not pay me back, family get-togethers became very awkward. *"Be not thou one of them that strike hands, or of them that are sureties for debts."* **Proverbs 22:26**

Many people are being squeezed by the stress of their debt and lack of financial discipline. They cannot get a good night's sleep without thinking about their debt. The bill collector is always calling and harassing them for the money that they have borrowed. It is not worth the stress; it is not worth the headache. Just as it pays to invest your money wisely, it also pays to make your debt payments on time. Take your life back by getting your financial house in order.

If you are going to live a CASH ONLY lifestyle know the difference between wants and needs. We all have those moments that after we have accumulated a little savings that we want to purchase a new car, new home or we just want to ball out. But, is this necessary? Sure, it would feel good for a moment. But, it doesn't benefit you financially in the long run. Instead of spending money on things that aren't practical, wealth builders put that money towards essential items that will continue to increase their wealth. If your destination is to join the financial elite club, it is going to require you to change your financial mindset and be discipline in your financial habits.

CASHOLOGY Quotes:

"It's time to get your financial house in order! - Wealth creation begins when YOU invest in your financial education." **Cashologist**

"Profits from can make you rich but earning interest and dividends from those profits can make you wealthy. Be smart with your money." **Cashologist**

"An investment in knowledge pays the best interest. Formal education will make you a living; an investment in self-education will make you a fortune." **Cashologist**

"There are NO SECRETS to wealth, it requires focus and discipline." **Cashologist**

"Once you know the rules to the financial game, you play it to your advantage. The power is in your hands." **Cashologist**

"The only difference between a rich person and poor person is how they use their time." **Cashologist**

"Spend less than you earn and invest the difference." **Cashologist**

"Today the greatest single source of wealth is between your ears." **Cashologist**

"Never spend your money before you have earned it." **Cashologist**

"You may have a fresh start financially at any moment YOU choose. Financial "failure" is not falling down, but staying down." **Cashologist**

> "All wealth has their origin in mind. Wealth is not an amount – it's an idea." **Cashologist**

CHAPTER II
THE PRINCIPLES OF BECOMING A CASHOLOGIST

If you are in debt, you are wasting massive amounts of money — money you ought to be utilizing to produce wealth for you and your family. So, paying off all your debt is absolutely a worthy goal. What a tremendous amount of stress we could have prevented if we were taught early in life the art of managing money, building wealth and avoiding unnecessary debt.

Debt is a Problem – It Puts YOU in Bondage

Debt that you are unable to pay back comes with a cost; your health which is affected by stress. And this is a very expensive price to pay for debt. Before you borrow or use a credit account, determine the cost of this transaction and whether you can afford the payments. If you are persuaded to submit an application for a credit card and you are presently finding it hard to pay your bills, then you need to stop and think about the decision that you are making. **Are you willing to give up your health and peace of mind for debt?**

Want to become wealthy and LIVE debt free? Then, manage your money wisely. **The key is financial literacy!** This is the cornerstone of any wealth-building program. It is far more important than the investments you make, how much you owe, or even the amount of income you earn. Manage wisely and you can become wealthy. Accumulate debt foolishly and you never will. If you want to be financially-smart, you have to be firm when it comes to living a CASH ONLY lifestyle.

Becoming debt free is a worthwhile goal. Some households actually maintain a debt free lifestyle. With a credit card, you have the power to buy whatever you desire at the spur of the moment and it is probably something you do not even need or perhaps, even want. You can save yourself a lot of heartache, by avoiding the following financial mistakes: having unrealistic expectations, being impatient and allowing your financial decisions to be influenced by other people who do not know how to manage their own finances.

Many of us can relate to making financial mistakes. In life, we can become consumed with trying to keep up with the Joneses. We acquire so much "stuff" we think will make us happy but in the end, it leads to emptiness because we are not grounded on sound financial principles.

When I took responsibility for the financial decisions I've made in life, I took back control. I could no longer blame the government, my job, or my parents. I knew I could either take responsibility or play the financial victim game. I realized that if I take the position of victim, I lose power. If I chose responsibility, then I would have the power to do something about the financial circumstances in my life. The more responsibility I accepted, the more power I attained.

It is Time to Take Responsibility for Your Financial Future

Your ideas and attitude about money and your finances will determine if you build wealth or live in debt. You have to think about your future. You need to start thinking about living financially-smart. A financial plan can help you reach your destination if you implement its strategies. A financial plan is one of the best tools you can use to live financially smart. The planning process can help you understand your financial goals and your strategies for achieving them. It leads you to face your financial fears and take action to living a CASH ONLY life. **The key:** is to put an end to the accumulation of debt and develop the habit of asset building.

The goal is to achieve financial freedom, free from debt and worry. It is not suggested that instead of owning credit cards, you load up your wallet with a bundle of cash. Of course, you can use debit cards and secured credit cards if you are certain that you have the money to cover the expenses. Most people dream about being financially free, but once they are required to make the necessary sacrifices, they stop dreaming. Be different. Do the hard work, and make solid plans to live by the CASH ONLY principles. Once you have the plans in place, act on them.

Many argue that since they work hard, they deserve to get whatever they want. But if you have to go into debt for those desires, then you are living outside of your means and you are purchasing those desires based on your future earnings which can lead to financial stress. When you make purchases using credit, the interest you are paying on that purchase is taking more money out of your pocket. People, who have the mindset of building wealth, always look for ways to get good returns on their money, not pay interest on non-appreciating assets.

At first, you may find it quite painful to not be free to buy whatever you want but over time, if you are smart with your money through saving and investing then eventually you will be able to pay for what you want with cash. Most people become wealthy and stay wealthy because they care as much about money going out as money coming in.

It takes discipline to get used to a CASH ONLY way of living. Wealth management is something you really have to devote time to in order to succeed. Either you give in and conform to the standards of a debt based lifestyle or stand your ground and stay away from unnecessary debt.

In life you will either be disciplined in your finances or have financial regrets. Being disciplined in your finances is a mental habit and you must choose the mental habits that empower you and serve you. What you focus on expands; if you focus on debt and how life is hard you will continue to experience unfavorable circumstances.

When you focus on living a CASH ONLY lifestyle, you will experience life more abundantly, because you will owe no one. The mind moves in the direction of its most dominant thoughts. You must choose to give power to circumstances, people and events that support you in living the life you desire.

Every decision you make with your money is an investment. Many people don't take the time to examine where their money is going and to make a conscious decision about whether it's going to worthwhile use. Know thy CASH FLOW!

To have control over your money and to become the master of money, you must develop a wealthy mindset and healthy financial habits. Wealth is a matter of expectation. **Our thoughts, feeling and attitude about money will always influence the outcome of our finances**. If we expect to do well in our finances then we will begin to think and act accordingly. Those that amass wealth create a habitual attitude and expectation of wealth.

We get in this life whatever we concentrate upon. Our financial success or financial failures is in our own hands. Many who are complaining that the door to financial success is locked by some mysterious person, or they have no one to help them to get the position they desire, are not succeeding financially because they are not willing to make the necessary effort to succeed.

They are not willing to do the work required; they want someone else to do the work for them to make things happen. **YOU do not have that excuse!** Through our experiences in life we have seen people who dreamed big dreams but failed to live out those dreams due to their halfhearted commitment to the process of developing themselves and the people that they surrounded themselves with. My mentor said; *"He could predict my financial future just by looking at the five people with whom I spend the most time with."*

To create wealth, you have to learn how to have self-control, have a financial plan and invest wisely. If you study the money habits of the wealthy, you will see a pattern. They only "use" other people's money to acquire assets such as real estate or businesses. This asset will pay back the money which was used initially and they will continue to earn income from that investment. In Robert Kiyosaki's bestselling book **Rich Dad Poor Dad**, he stated: *"Concentrate your efforts on only buying income-generating assets."* **Key principle:** Whatever you do with borrowed money, you should make more income and interest for you than what you have to pay back to the lender.

When you shift your mindset from a consumer to a wealth builder, you change to a new game with a new set of rules. When your mindset and habits about money change, your whole world starts changing. When you transform your thinking, you transform your world. There are no limits to you attaining your most desired financial goals as long as you can define what it is you want to achieve.

A great deal of what you have perceived as limits in your financial life are actually limits you have placed on yourself. The good news about this is that you have already begun to eliminate those limiting beliefs. **You began the moment you picked up this book!**

Challenge and change your mental programming. The secret of success is that the mind can accomplish whatever it believes. To be a wealth building informed investor, you must think like one.

Do not follow the path of those who blame everyone else for their financial woes and make excuses rather than take personal responsibility for their finances.

There are people, who live according to the wealth building principles, but there is an increasing number of people who lack basic financial skills and it is ruining their life. And it is our mission to change that. Financial literacy and the proper use of money is the key to creating a prosperous lifestyle.

CASH ONLY living begins not in a bank but in your mind. It begins with your thoughts. Throughout this book we are going to be working on your thinking. And this is very important. **No strategy will work in your life, business, or finances unless your thinking is right**. No one can think for you, all we can do is provide the necessary tools and it is your responsibility to take the steps to utilize them. To be successful at anything in life you must develop the right attitude. You may face some obstacles and setbacks but it is through your persistence and faith that you will achieve your financial goals.

CASH ONLY is not only a mindset, it is a lifestyle. You can quote affirmations all day, but it will not work without you taking action. In James 2:17 of the Bible it states, Faith without works is dead. It requires work and activity to succeed.

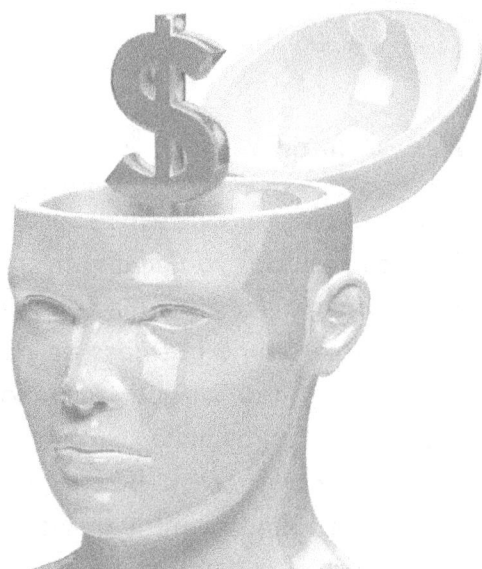

Applying The Wealth Principles of The Money Masters

The approach to wealth creation is different for many people. For a number of them, real estate investments offer a steady inflow of tax advantages and cash flow. To others, investing in the stock market is used as a strategy to increase their nest eggs.

Wealth comes to the man and woman who sees and uses his or her potential for wealth. Chances are that these men and women made a decision to set priorities, to pay themselves first and to build their economic power for the benefit of themselves and their family. In spite of what you believe wealth represents and what approaches you use in wealth creation, according to money masters, there are actually four principles of wealth creation:

• Increase income sources

• Earn more and spend less

• Start early

• Manage risks

What Is Your Source of Income?

When it is time to decide how you can earn more money, it can be difficult to weigh the options: do you spend more time at work earning overtime pay in trying to get a promotion and a higher salary, or do you invest time on a part-time business or passion where you can hustle in your free time and maybe earn some extra cash? Regardless of your personal circumstance, earning extra money is a key component to your financial success. Below are various sources and types of income to lay the foundation for this discussion.

Sources of Income

•**Primary Income (or Earned Income)** - The most common form of income is the money you earn by working a job. In return for your time and effort, your employer provides you with money in the form of a wage or a salary and/or a possible bonus. You are working for money. You must trade your time (a limited resource) for money. Once you stop working, the income stops coming in.

•**Passive Income (or Residual Income)** – This is income earned from sources other than your job. This can be money you earn from a side business such as network marketing, online business, real estate investment property or other projects. This is the opposite of earned income. Once you stop spending time on these income sources, the income flow do not necessarily stop. It is called passive income because you don't have to work a traditional nine-to-five hours to earn money. This kind of income is the key to wealth building and financial freedom. YOU earn money while you sleep.

•**Portfolio Income (or Investment Income)** - The money you make from interest, capital gains and dividends - "The money your money makes for YOU." Your money is working 24 hours for YOU!

To begin the process of building wealth, now is the time to think about how you can maximize your income-earning capabilities. Can you create a product that people will buy over and over again? Can you engage others to sell your product? How can you leverage your time to earn income off the efforts of others? The sooner you can answer these questions, the sooner you will have the potential to achieve financial freedom. Diversified income streams build wealth. Some of the wealthiest entrepreneurs have more than 10 income sources. You have to think like a wealthy person before you can become one.

Earn More and Spend Less

Launch your plans now. Dedicate at least two hours a day to a new venture or a business idea that will create a steady stream of passive or extra income. The key is to earn more and spend less. Establish concrete financial and personal goals for your family and your career. Unless you control your spending through the use of a budget, you will not be able to create wealth. I have worked with several people who have worked hard to build a healthy passive income, yet they failed to develop the habit of spending less than they earn. Too frequently, people who generate a million dollars per year end up with several million dollars in debt. **"Banks love to give money to people who don't need it."** Yet some people don't know how to control themselves when they have "access" to credit. Wealth builders hold down spending even as their earnings continue to grow.

Start Early

No matter where you are financially, today is always a good day to start looking for ways to earn extra and/or passive income. Don't expect to get wealthy through your standard job raises. What can your family really do with a 3% annual increase? On your journey to financial freedom, you have to radically increase your income and/or sources of income. You may have to change your career goals. You may have to step outside of your comfort zone and apply for the top position in your company. You may have to get rid of your cable T.V package, so that you can have some extra funds to invest in a new online business. Are you willing to do what is necessary to increase your income?

Manage Risks

Building wealth is largely about preserving your hard-earned assets. No wealth builder can afford to ignore risk. Risk management is part of everyone's life.

One unfortunate event in your life could wipe you out financially. Talking about wealth building is pointless until you have health insurance, because a single medical problem could bankrupt you. Health insurance must become one of your highest priorities. If your company doesn't offer it, buy it yourself. You can search online for information and quotes.

A change in your job can hurt your family financially, if you don't have reserves or other sources of income in place. Most people take action after catastrophe strikes. Don't let this happen to you. You've worked far too hard building up your assets to lose them. There has never been a better or more important time for YOU to apply the scout motto and 'be prepared'.

Activate CASH ONLY principles. Do not allow fear to cloud your determination to become financially free. Earn, save, and invest your money. Buy assets that will provide you with cash flow instead of purchasing liabilities. Make sound financial decisions. - CASH ONLY!

CASHOLOGY The Science Of CASH ONLY LIVING

Increase your sources of income and save at least 20% of your net pay every pay period. Never live on 100% of your income. Do not be one paycheck away from financial havoc.

Gain financial wealth building wisdom and take action. Read financial publications such as the Wall Street Journal, New York Times, Forbes, Money magazine, etc. Re-read this book once a quarter.

Before you make a purchase, ask yourself: "Is this a "want" or a "need?" Do not spend on needless things. Little expenses for seemingly insignificant purchases add up to large sums over time. You may not always make the right decision, but at least take the time to think before you make a purchase.

Have a financial purpose plan. Always have a long-term goal for your money. Save and invest your money with a purpose, whether it is to buy a house, investment properties, a business or retirement income. When your money has a purpose, you can live the life YOU want.

Give a portion of your income to a nonprofit charity or your house of worship. You decide on an amount of money that you feel you can sow into these ministries. All that matters is that the amount be meaningful to you and given with gratitude.

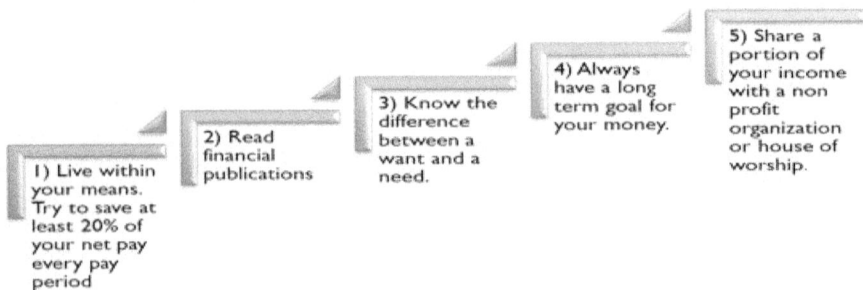

1) Live within your means. Try to save at least 20% of your net pay every pay period

2) Read financial publications

3) Know the difference between a want and a need.

4) Always have a long term goal for your money.

5) Share a portion of your income with a non profit organization or house of worship.

CASHOLOGY Quotes:

"If you make a living, if you earn your own money, you're free - however free one can be on this planet." **Cashologist**

"Financial success is a science; if you have the conditions, you get the result." **Cashologist**

"Don't wait for something big to occur. Start where you are, with what you have, and that will always lead you into something greater." **Cashologist**

"Doing what you love is fulfilling and leads to financial freedom." **Cashologist**

"If YOU get your attitude towards money straight, it will help straighten out almost every other area in your life." **Cashologist**

"Financial freedom is the progressive realization of predetermined, worthwhile, financial goals." **Cashologist**

"Financial failure will never overtake YOU if your determination to succeed is strong enough." **Cashologist**

"The only thing money gives you is the freedom of not worrying about money." **Cashologist**

"The wealth that you want also wants YOU. But you have to take action to get it." **Cashologist**

"Financial success is getting what you want. Happiness is wanting what you get." **Cashologist**

> "A major part of wealth building is having your heart and mind free from worry about the what-ifs of life."
> **Cashologist**

CHAPTER III
THE 10 CASH ONLY
COMMANDMENTS OF MONEY

We must seek and activate financial wisdom and understanding of the principles of money. It is going to take time and it is a process to gain full understanding of the principles, so you must be patient. You may be saying, "Wait a minute, I brought this book so I can get my financial house in order quick, I want my success today, as a matter of fact I want my success now." We understand and we have been there before, we had that same attitude at one point and it got us nowhere.

Today, many people function in an 'instant' mentality; they want everything instantly. Some so-called gurus may tell you that you can quantum leap to financial freedom, but my friend, it just does not work that way. The internet abounds with schemes offering you millions of dollars for basically sitting on your backside. Wealthy people find all this very amusing. The only one making money from those scams, is the person processing your credit card or cashing your check. It requires work to build wealth, and 90 percent of the work is on your thinking, attitude and beliefs about money.

Before you can see a change in your finances, you first have to change your thinking. There are no shortcuts to success.

Do you know why you want to be wealthy? Evaluate your definition of wealth and be realistic about how to build it and earn it. You must give yourself permission to be wealthy. You have to set a financial goal, write it down, make a plan and consistently work on that plan until you see the results. The more clearly your vision for financial freedom is, the closer you will move towards it and the closer it will move towards you. It's going to require work!

You must learn to take control and apply the principles that are necessary to become a wealth builder. When you begin living from your new money mindset, you start to make different decisions. You begin to associate with different kinds of people and you attract different circumstances into your life.

Warning: There will always be those who say that something cannot be done or worse, that you cannot do it. To fulfill your desire of CASH ONLY living requires an unwavering commitment to a goal that cannot be shaken by the negative uneducated comments of others. You cannot let others limit your thinking in what you desire to accomplish or what you can do. You must realize that other people can program you with their limiting thinking, so when people say things to you that are less than what you want, make a mental note that it is their opinion and not what is true. People will try to say what you qualify for and your level of ability.

You must at all cost, watch who you allow in your trusted circle of friends. By default, most people dwell on the negative – what they do not want to have happen – as opposed to the good things that could happen. This habit springs from social conditioning and past experiences. Many will be a distraction and you will have to limit your time with them as you travel on your financial journey. Financial freedom is within the reach of anyone who has a burning desire to achieve it and willing to put the work in.

Don't settle for mediocrity - Change! Either do nothing and let change happen to you, or find opportunities to make change work for you. It's your choice. Change affects your routine and your attitude.

Successful people don't succumb to procrastination or temporary distractions. Financial freedom is within the reach of anyone who has a burning desire to achieve it. You must be persistent and consistent in developing the habits of those who are already successful. However, it will not be easy; it will require some major adjustments in your thinking, beliefs and attitudes about money. For example, when my business partners and I first built our consulting business, in the beginning stages as a company, we were strapped for cash. Any cash flow we received was reinvested back into the business, and we knew that all the sacrifices we made were going to pay off. All of the executives, including myself, did not take a salary for the first two years.

Our desire for building a successful company was much greater than our short-term cash flow circumstances. We knew what we wanted, we created the vision, we developed the plan and we took action. All these things are important but if we did not have the desire that was strong enough to get us through those rough periods, we would have given up in the earlier stages. Goals, action plans, and outcomes are worthless without proper motivation.

There is nothing in life that can defeat you or deny you of success but yourself. Your own limiting thinking can defeat you; your lack of determination, indecisiveness and lack of confidence in yourself can defeat you but only if you let these negative attributes take hold. Pessimism is a learned behavior that can be changed. You have the power to change your conditions. Believe in yourself. Allow positive thinking to dominate your thoughts. Your success in life is up to you. Success will only come when you believe you deserve it. - *"According to your faith be it unto you."* **Matthew 9:29**

If you want to be successful, redirect the energy you put into making excuses for your financial setbacks, into making progress. YOU are your most valuable asset. By investing in your craft and developing your skills, you increase your worth and earnings potential. However, you need to commit to making this a priority throughout your life and wealth building journey. It is up to you to be all that you want to be, to do all that you want to do and to have all that you want to have. Life is about being, doing and having.

You are in charge. Think of your life as a movie. You are the writer, director, producer and star. You choose who gets to play a role in your movie. Whether the movie is a financial box office hit or a flop, it is in your hands. Your thoughts determine your outcome. If you think you are average, you are. If you think you cannot win, you will not. Conversely, if you see yourself succeeding, you will. If you expect great things to come into your life, they are on their way. When you lift yourself up, you lift up those close to you, too. The first and most important rule is to take responsibility for everything that happens in your life. Following this rule puts you in charge. Are you ready to command your future?

The key to living your life to the fullest is to never allow money to determine what you can and cannot do. Do not limit yourself and never allow a dollar to limit you either. Do not let your traditional thinking close your mind and prevent you from seeing the real truth: God wants you to prosper. God wants you to abound, and it is His blessing that enables you to accumulate wealth. God's basic desire for us is that we grow beyond simply being blessed and become a blessing to others.

"Beloved, I wish above all things that thou mayest prosper and be in health, even as thy soul prospereth." **3 John 2**

The accumulation of wealth is not a destination, but a journey. The people who have achieved financial freedom have paid the price on their journey. They stayed the course when others may have given up. Those who succeed in life commit to doing what they love and money will follow.

Financial success is not going to be handed to you; you have to challenge any self-defeating beliefs and take massive action. **How you think about money and what you believe tend to materialize in your life**. It is time to become a Money Master. If you want the same results as the wealthy, then you must take the necessary actions to create those results.

THE 10 CASH ONLY COMMANDMENTS OF MONEY

COMMANDMENT 1

Know Thy Source. Remember the LORD your God, for it is he who gives YOU the ability to produce wealth. When you are elevated financially, remember where your blessings come from. Avoid arrogance and be humble and grateful for the blessings God has bestowed upon you. Do not put your trust in money, but in the living God. "The blessing of the Lord, it maketh rich, and he added no sorrow with it." Proverbs 10:22 God is the source of your abundance. God has laid down a firm foundational plan to teach you how to become rich without sorrows. Keep in mind that these are God's words, not ours. God is the source, YOU are the asset and money is the servant. Never put a servant in the place of a master. God must come before money. If you spend five minutes a day seeking God's wisdom and eight hours a day chasing after money, then who or (what) is your source?

It is a matter of priority. Invest in your spiritual health to attain inner peace. Discipline yourself to separate your emotions from material things. God does not want to deprive you of the things you need to live, and to live abundantly. He just wants you to remember He is the source of it all. When you begin to experience the prosperous life, do not stop seeking God. As surely as you do, those things that God so richly blessed you with will begin to fall away. Part of your continuing success depends upon your recognition that God is your source. God is the one who supplies everything you need. With every upward advance in your wealth, learn to express gratitude. Give honor to God for the abundant harvest you are receiving.

COMMANDMENT II

*Master Thy Servant (Money). **Never allow money to decide what you can and cannot do**.* The first place to master money is in your mind. Wealth is created mentally first; it is thought out before it becomes a reality.

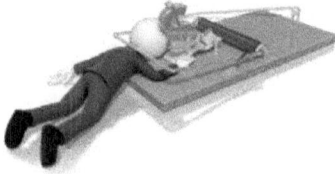

There are principles of economics that govern who will be wealthy and who will be broke. If we follow the principles that lead to wealth, we will be wealthy. We all play an important part in determining our own financial situations.

Have a positive attitude toward money; never allow money to determine what you can and cannot do. If you think too much about the lack of money or too much about your debt, all these things will tend to bring to you the very thing you are attempting to get away from. You can attract the things you desire as easily as you can attract the things that you hate and despise and long to get rid of. You can only rise and conquer your finances by lifting up your thoughts. When you operate within the laws of wealth, you will begin to experience life more abundantly and become the master of money.

COMMANDMENT III

Have A Storehouse To Manage Your Money. In order to manage your money, you need a storehouse. Carefully selecting a financial institution is probably the most important part of the process because selecting a bank that is a bad fit could mean you have to start your search all over again in a few months. That search should start with looking at what your priorities are for a checking, savings and investment account.

By knowing the cost and requirements for each of your accounts, it can save you the hassle and avoid unexpected fees. Every day we see various financial institutions waging war with their competitors. They try to offer us some incentive that will convince us to deposit our money with their bank. Some offer higher interest rates on money market accounts. Others offer free checking accounts with online banking. This is all nice, but you want to build a relationship with a financial institution that values you as a client.

Please realize that this commandment covers a very important issue. You see, if you do not have a storehouse to manage the finances in your life, no matter how much you seek to gain financial freedom, you will make no real progress towards building wealth.

COMMANDMENT IV

Know Thy Assets and Liabilities. Assets increase in value, liabilities decrease in value. An asset puts money into your pocket; an asset should generate income on a regular basis. Liabilities are the opposite of assets. Liabilities take money out of your pocket. Work to increase your assets and decrease your liabilities. Know the difference between good and bad debt.

What is good debt? When you use OPM (other people's money) to invest in an asset that provides a cash flow to pay back the debt, puts money in your pocket, and appreciates in value. These forms of debt "usually" have low interest rates and therefore can be maintained for long periods of time as you build up your assets. Bad debt includes debt you have taken on for things you do not need or cannot afford that decrease in value. The worst form of bad debt is consumer credit cards since they usually carry the highest interest rates. Interest rates for credit cards can far exceed even the best investments which would negatively impact your overall cash flow.

Most people get into money trouble because they don't exercise self-control. They want immediate gratification; they equate happiness with acquisition.

COMMANDMENT V

Know Where Thy CASH Flows. Measure your cash flow by tracking your weekly and monthly expenses versus your weekly and monthly income. Review your monthly bank statements, know where your cash is coming from and going to.

Take advantage of a number of services offered by your bank, including direct deposit and automatic bill pay. Make the most of online banking. To make the tracking of your expenses easy and accurate, pay for all your household expenses using one dedicated checking account. Grow your income more quickly than your expenses, so that each year you can devote more resources towards your long-term financial goals. Utilize your money with wisdom.

COMMANDMENT VI

Learn from Thy Fellow Money Masters. Seek out a mentor, someone who has already mastered money. Having mentors who have achieved success in their life is important to your success. Many have already traveled the road you may be on. I remember the advice from my mentor was: "Always learn from other people's mistakes and successes. It will save you time and money." Learn from those who have what you want; be a student of the financial game.

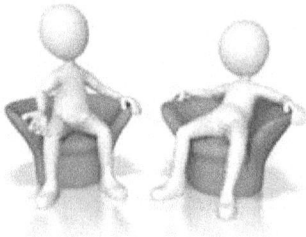

Consider joining with other money masters either in an internet community (CASH ONLY Online Community) or in a physical community.

Others with a similar mindset as your own can go a long way when it comes to helping you learn new financial skills, building your financial strengths, and identifying and overcoming your weaknesses. Read investing books, read the annual reports of the companies in your portfolio, and pay close attention to the news on Wall Street.

COMMANDMENT VII

Know Thy Friends. Do not waste your time discussing finances with someone who is not supportive of your financial education. You must stand on guard at the door of your thoughts; keep out all the enemies of your happiness and achievement.

"*The less you associate with some people, the more your life will improve. Any time you tolerate mediocrity in others, it increases your mediocrity.*" **Colin Powell**

We get so comfortable talking to the same people inside our circle of friends that we do not realize that how much we hear only supports our biases. Develop and expand your network; learn from those who are in position to help you achieve your goals. If you are not willing to learn, no one can help you. If you are determined to learn, no one can stop you. Build relationships with people who can help you grow, but don't be selfish, you must bring something to the table as well.

You cannot grow as long as you divide your loyalties with people, places and things that do not add-value to your life's mission.

COMMANDMENT VIII

Multiply Thy Streams of Income. Do not rely on one stream of income; if that one stream dries up, it can put you in a financial bind. Creating multiple streams of income ensures you will always be earning income. Creating multiple streams of income requires time, education, consistent work and commitment. If you want to earn more, work less and have financial freedom, you are going to have to start creating multiple income streams that do not require too much of your time. Release the traditional thinking of a "safe and secure job" and "playing it safe" behaviors. You will not be able to see the opportunities around you that could be a potential stream of income unless you are willing to learn from everything around you. Go to where the growth is and where you are able to bring in revenue. Do not chase after just any business; choose the business where you are able to grow and profit. You will gain financial freedom as well as time freedom.

COMMANDMENT IX

Owe No Man. The rich rule over the poor, and the borrower is servant to the lender. When you develop the habit of always borrowing money, you can be known as a leech. By having too much debt, it limits your chances of taking advantage of investment opportunities. Get intense, do away with your debt so that you may be free of those interest payments and start investing your money on the things that matter as you save for your future.

COMMANDMENT X

Spread the Wealth. Anything you hoard and keep that should be shared becomes your god. When you are generous and you spread your wealth to worthy causes, your giving allows God the opportunity to bless you. You are blessed to be a blessing.

When we are wealthy, our blessing is to be a blessing to others. You can never consider yourself wealthy if you do not have the heart to be generous with your money. As you give, so shall you receive. If you do not sow, you cannot reap. To have wealth in abundance, you must first begin to give, creating a new, life-changing flow to your wealth. Giving and receiving are interrelated and interdependent upon each other. People of means must recognize and be grateful for their extraordinary opportunity to provide long-term assistance to their fellow citizens. The power to influence and enrich the lives of others is a rare and precious gift that no one can afford to waste.

Schedule your giving. To turn a non-giver into a giver, talk about your giving. That often inspires others. Share your motivations and experiences.

Being a "wise" generous giver produces a positive, cooperative atmosphere all around you. In every aspect of life, receiving depends upon giving.

CASHOLOGY Quotes

"All money is a matter of belief." **Cashologist**

"Multiple streams of income is the key to financial freedom. Invest in your financial education." **Cashologist**

"Financial freedom is about becoming disciplined and using your money in a way that ensures you can live the sort of life you want both now and in the future." **Cashologist**

"What is your financial freedom number?" **Cashologist**

"A budget is your friend, when it comes to wealth building!" **Cashologist**

"Money is not bad. If you think it is, give ALL your bad money away. There's someone who can benefit from it....ME!" **Cashologist**

"People don't change when they feel good. They change when they're fed up. Pain pushes us to those crucial turning points. And, one day, enough will be enough! The question is, are YOU ready for a financial change?" **Cashologist**

"You may try to destroy wealth and find that all you have done is increase poverty." **Cashologist**

"Financial literacy is a work in progress. Nurture your financial independence." **Cashologist**

> "Your net worth to the world is usually determined by what remains after your bad habits are subtracted from your good ones." **Cashologist**

CHAPTER IV
THE WISDOM OF WEALTH

Many people misunderstand the idea of being wealthy. Many "try" to get rich by their own will power and human ingenuity. They gather up riches for themselves, but make a grave mistake of leaving out the most important things in life; they neglect their spiritual life, family and health. What is the point of wealth without health? **"Without health you will not enjoy your wealth."** What purpose is there to have all the wealth you desire but you do not have the health to enjoy it. Taking control of your health is of utmost importance because your body and mind are your most valuable assets and determine your well-being. **Do not let your net worth take the place of your self-worth. Your true wealth is priceless**.

Many may tend to equate financial success with material wealth. Even though these things can be an outward sign, they reflect only a small piece of the bigger picture that is your life. You could have all the money in the world, but if you do not have someone special to share it with, then it would be senseless. Life could be lonely without good people to experience it with. I just realized something, Benjamin Franklin, Andrew Jackson, Abraham Lincoln, or George Washington (money) never hugged me in the middle of the night. It would be scary if they did, but you know what I mean.

Money itself never guarantees happiness. If money guaranteed happiness, all the rich people would be abundantly happy and all broke people would be miserably unhappy. We know this is not the case. Rich people deal with life issues such as financial problems, drug addictions, death of a loved one and relationship challenges just as a broke person would.

Money simply does not guarantee happiness, but it also does not mean that you can neglect your financial responsibilities and live your life like a pauper. True happiness and lasting peace come through your relationship with God, your creator. When your relationship with God is right, your money will not cause you problems and unhappiness. Instead, it will be a blessing and a source of happiness for you and others around you.

Many make decisions in their pursuit for money that seem right but turn out to be deadly. Money must be put in its proper place. We all must guard our hearts, I love this quote by writer George Lorimer; "**It is good to have money and the things that money can buy, but it is good, too, to check up once in a while and make sure that you have not lost the things that money cannot buy.**"

We all must learn how to master money rather than be enslaved by it. Money is a good tool, if used properly. Money is to be regarded as a servant that comes to help and assist your life for prosperous living.

It is important to start shifting your mentality about money. In essence, the belief is that if you think of money with the right thoughts, you will attract money. On the other hand, if you are always worried about money, or even subconsciously reject the idea of having money, or think there is something wrong with wanting or believing that you deserve money, then you are pushing money away from you. Money is whatever you want it to be and means whatever you want it to mean.

"Cash is far more powerful in the hands of someone who knows how to invest it wisely, than someone who spends every dollar that touches their hand. Most people would not know what to do with a million dollars if it was handed to them." **CASH ONLY Strategist**

Confront your own feelings about money. Many are unaware of the wealth that is available to them. Some believe they do not deserve to have wealth. Then there are those who believe that to deny oneself of wealth is noble. There is nothing noble about living in lack, not knowing how you are going to pay your bills or feed your family. Go tell someone who is unable to provide for their family that it is noble for their children to be hungry. Make sure you run after you make that statement.

Traditional erroneous teachings have some people believing that God does not want His children to be wealthy. I've never subscribed to that way of thinking and I advise you not to, as well. I believe we all deserve to be wealthy!

The 9 Money Languages

What Money Language, Do You Currently Speak?

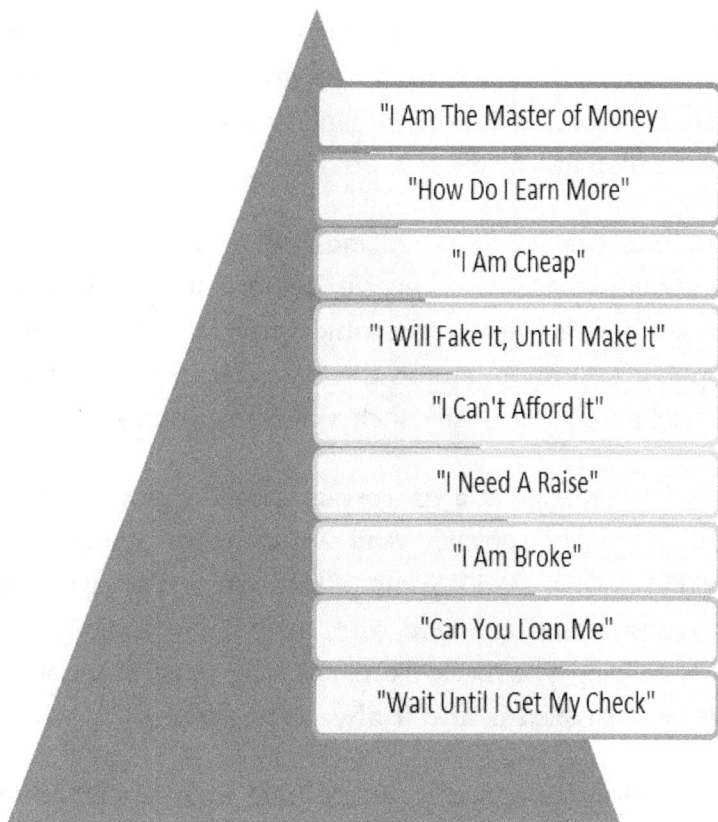

"I Am The Master of Money

"How Do I Earn More"

"I Am Cheap"

"I Will Fake It, Until I Make It"

"I Can't Afford It"

"I Need A Raise"

"I Am Broke"

"Can You Loan Me"

"Wait Until I Get My Check"

Money Languages: What Language Do You Speak?

Our money language is passed down from generation to generation. We learn the language of money by what we hear from our parents, friends, teachers, religious beliefs, musical influences and everything in our environment. Think back to the phrases that you heard as a child. What do you recall? Phrases such as, "that is too expensive," "we cannot afford that" and other similar utterances may be familiar to many people. Your memories about money will tell you a great deal about how you were influenced by those around you and whether those memories still influence how you handle money today.

Frankly, nobody ever sat us down and gave us the knowledge we needed to learn about wealth. We receive no formal education in the most critical of all life skills - how to become wealthy. Did you ever, in all your years of public education, attend the class: The 9 Money Languages? Or Wealth building 101? Why isn't such a class mandatory in every school?

This lack of knowledge is a dangerous situation, since money is one of life's most important subjects. And we all need money to survive and move around on this world. Some of life's greatest enjoyments and most of life's greatest disappointments stem from your decisions about money. No one is holding you back from changing your financial future. **The power is in your hands and it always has been.**

There are 9 Money Languages, we all have experienced or used at one point in our life. I know I used every last one of them. I'm not going to fake the funk and say I was always wealthy. I'm transparent about my financial journey.

With money, YOU determine the language you want to speak. As we go through the 9 Money Languages, I want you to be honest with yourself. If you don't like the money language you currently speak, you can always learn a new one.

"Wait Until I Get My Check" This money language is spoken by those who always seem to have to wait until they receive a paycheck to make any kind of purchase. When you hear "Wait until I get my check," you know what money language this person speaks. We call this the living from paycheck to paycheck language of money. We all may have started out from this position at one point in our lives or at the start of our careers. I recall when I was working as a security guard, my mindset at that time was a paycheck mindset. I only made enough income to get to and from work. My friends would ask me to go out with them on a weekend vacation but at that time, I did not have the discipline to put money aside for any outside ventures.

The honest answer was that I did not set any money aside for savings, investing, or retirement. I barely was able to pay my monthly obligations. I developed the habit of speaking the money language of "Wait until I get my paycheck." It was a struggle to break this money language. I had to change my financial habits.

I had to learn to set aside a portion of my income, despite the circumstances of not earning enough. In order to break free from the paycheck to paycheck lifestyle, one must become sick and tired of being sick and tired of this lifestyle. Until this money language becomes uncomfortable, people will continue to live as an underearner.

How do I change my "wait until I get my check" money language? You first must change the way you think about money. What type of relationship do you have with your money? Is it an appreciative relationship or are you frustrated by your lack of it? As you learn more about your money beliefs, you will gain more of an understanding about your money habits. Create a list of your financial priorities. It is very important that you know exactly where your money is going, who is getting paid and how much interest you are paying. Begin tracking all of your spending on a daily basis; know where thy cash is flowing.

Begin to use cash or your debit card instead of using your credit card. The key is to not accumulate any debt and to know what you are spending your money on. Change your thinking, so that saving cash becomes a source of satisfaction. As your savings grow, you'll have the funds to invest in income producing opportunities. Alleviating your worry about money leads to personal satisfaction.

Saving at least 20% of your paycheck is fundamental to breaking the cycle of living paycheck to paycheck because you are putting yourself in a position to build wealth. You must make paying yourself first a priority. You can make your first payment from your earnings in the form of an automatic deposit to your wealth building account. If you have extra cash coming in and you are consistent in paying your 20% to yourself then by all means, add more to your wealth building account.

"Can You Loan Me?" Although, some people are responsible enough to pay back what they borrow, some are habitual borrowers.

This money language is spoken by those who are always looking for a hand out. Always taking and never giving. They promise to pay you back, but you can never find them or hear from them until they need to borrow again. We call this the borrower's language of money.

Who wants to be a person who pays their bills late, receive handouts from others or be a person who is always owing and not owning?

You probably have some people in your life at this moment you know who speak this money language. These people are always asking for loans and know how to manipulate others. They make people feel guilty when they tell them "no." Excuses are all these people make for not having any money. It requires work to break a beggar's mentality.

A strong accountability group is needed, because people who speak this money language look for people who enable them, and they can easily take advantage of. If you speak the "Can you loan me?" money language and many will deny it, know that your mentality is a hindrance to you experiencing true financial freedom.

How do I change my "Can you loan me?" money language?
First, call everyone that you owe money to and tell them that you have decided to pay back all you have borrowed. Don't just "say" you're going to repay them, actually make the effort and do it. So, list all of your debt obligations and arrange them in order from the smallest balance to the largest. Begin with the smallest balance by putting as much as you can above and beyond the minimal amount toward your payment.

When you finish paying off the debt, then celebrate! Celebrate the fact that you are no longer a slave to your lender. You have now elevated from "Can you loan me?" to "I have so much to give, who can I help?" Givers always gain! This is an awesome way to move your mindset from personally being helped to putting away a portion of your income to help and empower others.

When you change your mindset from helping "Me and mines and no more" to "My giving will be changing the future of generations to come," you have now elevated your language of money and your use of money. You have now risen to putting your money and yourself in the position of inspiration.

"I Am Broke" Being broke is not a pleasant experience. The morale of a person who is always broke is one that is fragile. Their insecurity regarding finances is brought to light during financial conversations. People who speak the "I Am Broke" money language claim to never have any money but always seem to be buying things. They spend a great deal of time at the local malls shopping, yet never have any money to spare. We call this the broke person's mentality of money.

Being broke is a temporary state of being. In my earlier working years, I lived in this temporary state of being broke for a while. No matter how hard I worked, it always seemed that I did not have enough money. I heard the older folks say: "The harder you work, the more you make." I am not saying they did not know what they were talking about, but this type of advice did not work for me. I worked from 8 until faint and still, my bank account had the same $3.00 at the end of the month.

How do I change my "I am broke" money language?

When I started to work smart and save my money, I began to see a change in my finances. I first created a tracking sheet to see where my money was going, because it sure was not going into my bank account. I noticed that I was spending a large portion of my income on eating at restaurants while I was at work. The harder I worked, the hungrier I got and the more I spent my money.

To rectify my use of money, I shifted my spending habits at work. Instead of buying lunch, I brought my lunch from home. Let me be honest here… my wife forced me into eating leftovers and it paid off. I went from being broke to having surplus; I was saving an additional $500 a month just by eating leftovers.

So, at the end of the month, there was $503 in the account to go towards saving and investing. My financially-disciplined life paid off and is still serving me well to this day. I'm a long way from having a $3 balance in my account.

"I Need A Raise" This is the "needy" money language; this individual is always expecting something. They also believe more money is going to solve their money problems. They believe that by trading more of their time, they should receive more money. Now consider this: the average annual pay raise is about 0.5-2%. Is your time worth more than 0.5%? I am not advising you to deny yourself a raise or not accept it.

My advice to you is to never allow a raise to suppress the creative spirit in you. There is a creative idea on the inside of you that can yield more income than that raise you are seeking. When I was working, I used to think that a raise would help me. Yet when they gave me that raise of $1.50, I would just get upset. I would have to work much harder for that $1.50 and inevitably, the cost of living would go up and I ended up back where I started in terms of my income not being able to meet the needs of my expenses.

How do I change my "I need a raise" money language? When you settle for a job that you dislike, you suppress or exchange your creativity for a paycheck. You can get trapped into the idea of always looking forward to your next annual 2% pay raise and missing your creative voice telling you that you can do better or be earning more by doing something that you enjoy. Do what you love and you'll never work another day in your life. Always give yourself a raise because no one else will ever give you the raise you deserve. If you are creative, look for ways you can increase your income. Make a list of things you can do that can provide some extra income and not require a great deal of your time. For example, if your spouse has asked you to clean the cluttered garage for the past two years, use this opportunity to have a garage sale.

"I Can't Afford It" This money language is spoken by those who know the price of everything and yet are unable to determine the value of anything.

This person allows money to determine what they can and cannot do. Instead of creatively devising a way to attain the money needed to buy the item, this person would rather put it out of their mind all together. This person knows what they want and yet automatically feels like they do not deserve it. They place too much value on the price instead of what they want. It almost seems like they have thoughts of unworthiness. They are the only one who can change these kinds of limiting beliefs and come to a sense of worthiness within their self.

How can I change my "I can't afford it" money language? When you ask yourself, "How Can I Afford It?" you are now setting your mind in motion to make your dream of attainment become reality. I am not advocating going out to purchase items that have no value, like clothes that you wear one time or hang in your closet with the tag on. Rather, I am promoting that you open your mind to the possibilities of attaining items that will add to your wealth and have some form of resale value. The point is to ask yourself: "How can I afford it?" and then, "What is my plan of action after I attain it?"

"I Will Fake It Until I Make It" This may surprise you that this is a money language. You have many financial gurus who say the best way to make yourself believe that you are rich is to fake it until you make it. These individuals are the best dressed at every social gathering. They buy expensive items on credit. They look good and smell good but owe everybody. You look inside their closets and they have a closet full of knock off products. Their watch is supposed to be a Rolex but since it is an imitation: it says Nolex. Do not fake it!

How can I change my "I will fake it until I make it" money language? If you are the faker and owe everyone in town, your credibility is probably already nonexistent. By being fake, you are not being true to yourself. You become more concerned about what people think of you. And living for other people's approval keeps you in bondage. You know what happens when you try to keep up with the Joneses. If this is you, I encourage you to live realistically. You do not need to impress anyone but yourself. This act of courage on your part will show that you have self-respect.

It is good to wait until you have more than enough cash flow and you have your financial house in order so that you may be able to purchase the real thing. **Being authentic is the only way to live!**

"I Am Cheap" This money language is spoken by those who may have money but are too scared to part with it. Being cheap has nothing to do with how much money you have. You can be rich and cheap, or broke and cheap. People who are cheap buy everything at the second-hand stores and spend hours of the day clipping coupons in efforts to hoard their money. They are the ones who run to the bathroom when the bill comes when you are eating at the restaurant or they will pull out their calculator and start crunching numbers on their portion of the meal. Let me make this clear: there is nothing wrong in clipping coupons to get extra savings or a discount. Give me a pair of scissors and some coupons I will be clipping to save those dollars.

The "I Am Cheap" mentality/language becomes a problem when the ultimate result is the hoarding of money.

How do I change my "I am cheap" money language? As stated earlier in this book, much of the money language habits are learned from childhood. If you speak and live the "I Am Cheap" money language, it may be because you were a person who may have grown up poor and did not have much. Then when you began to earn money, you were constantly reminding yourself of when you had to do without because of the lack of money. You end up placing a great deal of value on money; you believe the money is going to save you from poverty when poverty has more to do with a mindset. You must forgive your past, realizing that the past is not the present and does not equal the future.

Make a choice to enjoy your life. Be smart, not cheap. Enjoy your money before you leave this earth because if you don't, someone else is going to enjoy spending your money doing fun things.

"How Can I Earn More?" This money language is spoken by the creators in society. This group looks to earn money; they are not looking for handouts. They earn money and continue the process of earning more money through their creative use of ideas.

They are always looking for opportunities and ways to add value and solve the problems of the masses. If the person is not satisfied with their current income they look for opportunities to expand, either through creative ideas or business opportunities.

The creators in society are innovative in their thinking.

If you have an idea that you believe will add value to peoples' lives, you should do whatever it takes to make it become a reality. There are people ready and willing to invest money in a good business idea. Someone believed in Bill Gates' vision for Microsoft and they received a wonderful return on their investment.

How can I earn more? If you are passionate about your idea and you believe in it, do your due diligence by writing a business plan. When your business plan is professionally completed, you can now market your business idea to potential investors. If you are finding it difficult to find adequate financing, you may want to consider finding another source of income to finance your own idea to make your dream a reality.

"I Am the Master of Money" This is the most sophisticated money language where leverage is power. This is when CASH ONLY is the mindset and the lifestyle. Those who speak this money language know that their earning potential is unlimited. They invest their time and money in the creators of society. We call this the mastery level of the language of money.

To reach the money language mastery level, one must have enough useable income to invest in other businesses or startups. These types of investment vehicles can exponentially increase your earning power, provided that you have done your due diligence in your choice of business investment. These investments will continue to yield income for you as long as the business is lucrative. If you desire to reach this level of Money Mastery, speak to someone who has demonstrated sound financial decisions in their life.

When you do what wealthy people do, you create wealth. Wealthy people understand that abundance comes from enriching others. Becoming wealthy takes hard work. Be prepared to put in the necessary time and effort. **Keep pressing forward with financial wisdom and surely you will achieve this Money Mastery language**.

CASHOLOGY Quotes

"Are YOU a spender, saver, or investor?" **Cashologist**

"The major key to financial failure is trying to impress people with things you bought on credit. What is more impressive is to buy assets using cash and owing it outright." **Cashologist**

"The road to wealth and debt travel in two different directions. - Which road are YOU traveling on?" **Cashologist**

"If you are serious about being wealthy, you will have to learn how the wealthy think." **Cashologist**

"No strategy will work in your life, business, or finances unless your thinking is right." **Cashologist**

"Wealth is a product of the creative mind. The mind that fears, doubts, depreciates its power, is a negative, non-creative mind, one that repels wealth, repels supply. It has nothing in common with abundance, hence cannot attract it." **Cashologist**

"There are no short cuts to financial "freedom" - YOU must put in the work." **Cashologist**

"Wealth is not an amount, it's an idea." **Cashologist**

"Even if you grew up around wealth, you still have to learn the PROCESS of how to handle and maintain wealth. No one is exempt from learning the wealth process." **Cashologist**

Chapter V
The Seven Step To Financial Freedom

We all have the right to pursue peace, happiness, and the path of prosperity. Wealth, like any other skill, needs to be learned. Don't ever think you know everything. Don't ever stop learning. Enjoy the process. You can enjoy the power of becoming financially independent if you make a decision to invest wisely, develop short term and long term financial goals, and circulate your wealth with a purpose.

There is a shocking truth about wealth. Wealth adores a person who has a healthy attitude towards it. **Thoughts of your mind have made you what you are, and the thoughts of your mind will make you whatever you become from this day forward**. Once you realize this, you will come to a full understanding that people, places, conditions, and events cannot keep wealth from coming to you.

We all have the freedom to "choose" to be wealthy. We can enjoy the feeling of being free and knowing that we are giving that sort of heritage to our children. You are changing your family legacy when you decide to be free from the bondage of debt. You are going from a debt system to a wealth building lifestyle.

"No one is in control of your financial future but you; therefore, you have the power to change anything about yourself or your financial habits that you want to change." **Cashologist**

Today is the day you need to take action in regards to whatever financial situation you may be in. You have the power to eliminate all financial pressures and discover the joy of financial freedom. It begins with self-discipline, and a vision. Begin to see yourself financially free, allow this to propel and motivate you to action. A positive attitude that arises from a firm belief that you can succeed is essential. But action is also mandatory.

We have entered a critical time in history: the financial stability of our family is now our responsibility. It is the time to get serious about you and your family's financial stability. Are you committed? This is not for the fainthearted. You need a burning desire and a commitment to act. **To not make a commitment is to commit to do nothing.**

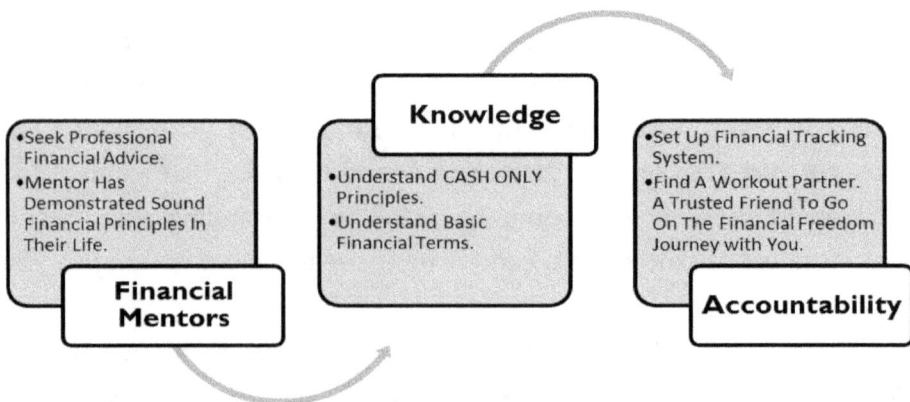

Knowledge
•Understand CASH ONLY Principles.
•Understand Basic Financial Terms.

•Seek Professional Financial Advice.
•Mentor Has Demonstrated Sound Financial Principles In Their Life.
Financial Mentors

•Set Up Financial Tracking System.
•Find A Workout Partner. A Trusted Friend To Go On The Financial Freedom Journey with You.
Accountability

Got a Financial Plan?

Many people get nervous when they hear the word "financial plan" because they do not have a full understanding of it. Having a plan for your finances is the most important thing you can do to help you be financially successful. The basic idea behind financial planning is to save and invest money with a purpose.

I have heard people whine about being too busy with their daily routine to create a financial plan; they barely have time to plan for a better life today, much less look ahead. The truth is, these people are too lazy to make necessary changes. Sometime in the past these individuals stopped playing to win and started playing not to lose and now they are losing big time. Fear of failure, peer pressure and discomfort at the thought of leaving their routine lulled them to settle instead of stepping outside of their comfort zone. They'd rather spend 8 to 10 hours on a job they do not like and then come home and spend 4 hours in front of the idiot box (TV) in an attempt to escape their mental prison.

Never stop changing, adapting or plugging away at financial success, and you'll never stop finding ways to get ahead. Many people would live a wonderful life if they knew how to manage their money and track their expenses. There are many people who make a great deal of money but are broke because they do not manage their money well. With a financial plan, you have the tools to decide exactly what is going to happen with your earned income.

Recognize that you have all the tools necessary to accomplish what you want financially. You must become good at planning and each and every day, you must work your financial plan by setting priorities to accomplish your financial goals. It is extremely important to know how much money you have to circulate, to save and invest.

Seek counsel from someone who has demonstrated sound financial discipline in their life. It is important to your financial future that you know you are headed in the right financial direction. If you are completely honest with yourself, a financial plan is the guide to let you know your success.

It does not matter how much money you make, it is how much you keep that counts. If you do not learn and develop the financial discipline that would make your money work for you, you will have a hard time building wealth. Wealth builders consistently place themselves in the path of opportunity and make probability work in their favor when it presents itself. To get to the level of having financial freedom, you must take control of your finances, and it requires the right financial habits.

Remember that no one will care more about your financial future than you. Begin to create a plan of action today that will convert your financial dreams into reality. You may want to start subscribing to financial publications such as Forbes, Money or Fortune. Also choose to read the Wall Street Journal instead of the trash news.

History is often written by people who believe in a dream so intensely that they are willing to commit themselves totally to the realization of that dream. You have probably heard it said before that it is impossible to succeed without believing. In other words, if you want to succeed in life, then you must believe in what you are doing. It is called faith and with it, your possibilities in life are limitless. Without faith, the complete opposite is true; you will travel down a pathway of frustration and setbacks every time.

Constantly expand your knowledge, your range of skills and your network of contacts so you can stay "relevant" – able to contend with whatever the future bring forth. Change will come regardless of what you do or don't do. You only control whether you are ready for it and how you respond to it.

"There is no such thing as financial failure, only the price of an education."
Cashologist

Being wise with your money is a process, step by step not a one-time all or nothing dash for the cash. As you make a firm decision to become financially free, you must have a builder's mentality and a blueprint for your financial goals. You do not have to take unnecessary risks to be financially successful. Once you have a plan of action to earn your first million, acquiring the second million is much easier. To broaden your financial thoughts, T. Boone Picken stated: *"The First Billion is the Hardest."* The difference between those who achieved true financial success and those who continue to struggle, no matter how much money is coming into their home, is based on the possession of a wealthy mindset. Wealthy people have a dream that they are committed to, and they continue to work at it until it becomes a reality.

Have you paid yourself today? Do you save 20% of everything you earn? I do not believe it to be sensible to work a full week and as soon as you receive your check, you give it all away to pay bills. You need to develop the habit of paying yourself first. Every time you are paid for services rendered, make sure you keep a portion of that income to invest for you and your family.

Declare: A portion of my income is mine to keep to invest in my financial freedom.

We who have worked to achieved financial success, believe and know we deserve to keep a portion of all we earn. We are unwilling to rely on others or circumstances to determine our financial future. We gain an understanding of the financial principles, obtain assets and create the circumstances for our own success. We make things happen rather than simply waiting for something to happen.

When you pay your bills, the first check you must write is to yourself. Always pay yourself first – prior to spending any money, make that sacrifice to pay yourself first and from this, you should put away some in an investment plan and also your savings. Consider yourself as a bill to yourself; pay that bill and deposit that money in your financial freedom account. Pay yourself first even if you believe you cannot afford it. The truth is, you cannot afford not to. Pay that money to yourself even if you have to cut that cable bill. The time you spend mesmerized by someone else's life on television you can be using to create the magnificent new life that will make others stand in awe. Be Wealthy! Go ahead; I dare you!

Learn and take action. It really does not matter where you were or where you are now; it matters where you are going. Our desire is for you to begin setting financial goals to achieve results. These goals may be either short-term or long-term. Long-term goals can take about three to five years to achieve, while short-term goals are attainable within six months to three years. Short-term goals are often a stop along the way to your long term goals.

The right way to set and achieve your financial goals: S.M.A.R.T.

People routinely make commitments about accomplishing major goals and changing their habits: earning more money, getting a promotion, losing weight, being better in their relationship – and then fail to fulfill them. However, some people do keep their commitment to themselves and achieve their goals. They succeed because they set demanding goals that motivate, challenge and inspire them. Everyone carries the seeds of greatness.

Specific. Your goals must be desirable, something you want to accomplish. This is the Who? What? When? and Why?

Set specific goals. Most people have goals to be successful, get rich, improve relationships and the like, but these are very vague and the mind can become confused. If we can imagine something, see it or picture it, we're a lot more likely to process, understand and embrace it. Visualize your goals. The better you are able to do this the easier it is for your subconscious to embrace your goals. Specific goals like "I will earn $500,000 by the end of this year," or "I will become the sales manager of the sales division by next month," or "I will invest in my marriage, so my spouse and I will attend a marriage retreat twice a year." are much more effective and allow you to measure your progress. Include the amount, position name, and the date and all the important details needed to train your mind to start working towards that goal. If you want results that you can be proud of, be specific.

Measurable. How do I know if I met my goals? What am I doing to track my progress?

Goals need to be measurable so that you can gauge how well you are doing. To help measure your paths and goals, you should include measurable details.

69

For your job, you can include details such as the number of hours you are working, the amount you are earning, the staff you are handling, etc. For your financial goals, you can include details such as the amount you want to have as a whole or the amount you want to earn on a monthly basis. Always have important points and items to be measured so you can understand how close you are to achieving your goals. If your goal is to earn $50,000 a month, then you know you are halfway there if you're already earning $25,000 a month. But how do you get to $50,000 a month?

Attainable. Your goals must be achievable.

In the beginning stages of setting goals, some people set goals that are so high to reach that they are almost setting up things that may be challenging to achieve. It is ok to set challenging goals, just make sure you set objectives that you can reach within a given amount of time, provided the current resources and capabilities you have. Some goals can be achieved faster compared to others if you have the knowledge and skills to pursue them. When you list your goals, and start devising a plan to reach them, goals become more attainable because you are focused. Each day, ask yourself, "What must I accomplish today in order to know that I'm on track" to achieve my goals?

Realistic. Your goals must be believable to YOU!

Goals should be challenging, but also realistic. The best way to set goals is to set a parameter outside of your comfort zone – but not so far outside that it seems wildly impossible. Goal-setting should be aspirational so do not be afraid to think big and reach for your goals. At the same time, make sure you are empowered and equipped to achieve your goals. Such ambitious goals probably will make you feel fearful at some point. Be prepared to deal with these emotions. Your plans and goals can be destroyed by fear. Take the time to identify and understand your fears. An excellent way to overcome fear is by taking action.

Fear disappears once you start to do something. Keep fear from affecting your motivation to accomplishing your goals. Believing in yourself is vital to attaining any goal.

Time. Your goals must have a timetable, a specific time frame to reach your goal. **Time will either promote you or expose you.**

You must feel a sense of urgency about your goals or they will never happen. Setting the exact time and date will spur you to start working on your goals instead of putting it off for another day. Some goals can take years to accomplish so it is wiser to break them down into smaller objectives. Each day, ask yourself, "What did I do today to advance my goals?"

The key is: You must act on your goals every day. For the next 30 days, review the financial goals you have set for yourself. Review your goals every morning, throughout the day, and during the evening. Force your goals into your subconscious mind; see yourself as already having attained them. Like repetition, visualization is a technique you can use to get what you want. Do this consistently every day for the next 30 days and it will become a habit. A habit that will lead you from one success to another all the days of your life.

"Good financial habits are the key to success. Bad financial habits are the unlocked door to failure. I will form good financial habits and become their slaves." **Cashologist**

7 Steps to Financial Freedom

Here is a seven-step goal-setting exercise that you can use to set and achieve your financial goals. These action steps summarize the best techniques for setting goals, streamlining your activities, and enabling you to accomplish vastly more than the average person.

Step No.1: Know your financial freedom number.

You need to know exactly what amount you will need coming in, passively on a monthly basis, passively that would give you financial freedom.

Write down a specific dollar amount that you feel you will need to live a comfortable life. This is for you and your family; you do not need anyone's approval about how small or large this number should be.

Financial planning and goal-setting are long-term commitments we make to ourselves and family. A good way to start is to identify both your short-term and long-term goals. If your financial freedom number is $500,000 per year, then stick with it and do not deviate from it.

Step No. 2: Have a reason why and know how it would make you feel to achieve your financial goal.

Goals

1. _____
2. _____
3. _____

Your reason: **Why?** must be much bigger than just paying your bills. Your "why" must motivate you, because you must become more to earn more. It will be a process you must go through before you achieve your goal.

If you have the expectation to be a millionaire, know that it is going to take some time, especially if you have never made more than $100,000 dollars in a given year or month.

Step No. 3: Evaluate the obstacles that you will have to overcome to achieve your financial goal.

Once you decide to be financially free, take consistent and persistent action. There will be obstacles you will need to overcome. For example, if you are a compulsive spender, you may need to stay away from the local shopping malls until you overcome your spending habits.

Eliminate any self-defeating obstacles that will hinder you from achieving your goal. Stick to your commitment. You have great potential. But you need to focus on clear goals. No matter where you start, know where you are going. You can get there. You are what you think, or you can be what you think. Change what you think about to change what you are.

Step No. 4: You will need the proper tools that will empower you to have the skills and abilities needed to reach your financial goal.

In order to achieve a financial goal that you have never reached before, you must develop knowledge and necessary skills needed to accomplish that financial goal. Jim Rohn, America's foremost business philosopher, said: *"After you become a millionaire, you can give all of your money away because what's important is not the million dollars; what's important is the person you have become in the process of becoming a millionaire."*

Every new goal requires that you become a new person, in some way, by developing additional knowledge and skills in order both to achieve it and to keep it.

Step No. 5: Evaluate your associations. The people you surround yourself with will determine if you achieve your financial goal.

Achieving financial freedom requires the active cooperation of many people. Remember, it is all about relationships. Seek out those who have already achieved financial freedom. Do not be afraid to ask for help, even if it is in the form of advice and introductions from the people you know.

Build your relationships and choose your friends carefully.

One person, one contact, can make all the difference between success and failure. Avoid negativity, including negative individuals who want to bring you down. Such people work against your best interests.

Step No. 6: Create a plan to achieve your financial goal.

Put your plan in writing and review it daily. Your plan becomes your compass to keep you on track. Make a list of your financial obligations. Organize the list into a plan based on priority and sequence.

Everyone's financial freedom goal might be slightly different. Some might be content with their finances but are failing to plan for their children's college education or to put aside for their 401k or retirement. Whatever your inner voice is telling you to improve on is what needs to drive your passion.

Step No. 7: Take Action!

Once you begin, never stop. Do something every day that moves you toward the achievement of your financial goal. Every day presents you with choices, and you have power over how your life can unfold. Remain focused on all the worthy aspects of your life. Don't get bogged down by what you don't have or where you fall short. Concentrate on the people and things that you consider your blessings. When the going gets tough, stay focused. It isn't what happens to you, but how you cope with what happens that determines your success.

Develop a bias for action and a sense of urgency. Be persistent and consistent moving towards your goal. Do whatever is necessary once you begin working on your goal; never stop until you achieve it. Get the results you desire. Breaking old beliefs and habits is dependent upon noticing them as the barriers to success that they are. To accelerate the process of achieving your financial goal, create a clear mental picture of what your goal would look like as if you had already achieved it.

Begin with the end in mind. Your overall success is determined by what you choose to focus on the most in the world from day to day. That's the key.

Visualize and imagine your goal as a reality. Imagine the feeling of joy and satisfaction you would feel if the goal was accomplished.

Journal your experience to achieving financial freedom. Then you will have a blueprint for others to follow. This will change your family's legacy.

Throughout history, the world's most successful people have used techniques like these to get what they want. These methods will work for you, regardless of your circumstances or what you may be up against. Your main job is to be absolutely clear about what it is you want, make a plan to achieve that goal, and then to think about it and work on it every single day. Remember, there are no limits except the limits you place on your own imagination.

Master These Wealth Building Skills

- Get in the habit of paying yourself first
- Save 20% of all income
- Begin paying for things with CASH ONLY
- Learn to how to read a financial statement
- Accumulate assets, not liabilities
- Learn to protect your assets
- Study the global financial markets
- Put yourself in the position to have interest work in your favor and not against you. Be the lender, not the borrower
- Have your money work for you bringing in more money Money-Making Money!!!

CASHOLOGY Quotes:

"Believe in yourself! Have faith in your abilities! Without a humble but reasonable confidence in your own powers you cannot be successful or build wealth" **Cashologist**

"Wealth is a way of living and thinking, and not just money or things. Poverty is a way of living and thinking, and not just a lack of money or things." **Cashologist**

"If you don't design your own financial plan, chances are you'll become a burden in someone else's plan." **Cashologist**

"Strong, deeply rooted desire is the starting point for building wealth." **Cashologist**

"I think there is something, more important than believing: Action! The world is full of leaders. There aren't enough who will move ahead and begin to take concrete steps to actualize their vision." **Cashologist**

"Change before you have to." **Cashologist**

"Most people struggle financially simply because they haven't paid the price to decide what is really important to them." **Cashologist**

"Ordinary riches can be stolen; real wealth cannot. In your soul are infinitely precious things that cannot be taken from you." **Cashologist**

I_____ on _____
am making a vow to use **CASH ONLY** so that I may change my life, create wealth and live free from the bondage of debt.

I will think and activate **CASH ONLY** principles every day of my life.

I will be the example and teach others **CASH ONLY** strategies.

I will promote and help create a **CASH ONLY** community.

All successful people know what they want. They set goals and write them down. This book is based on creating a CASH ONLY lifestyle, the following will be focusing on financial goals. "...without a vision the people perish." Proverbs 29:18

Do you have the mindset and correct money habits to be wealthy? Yes/ No - Why?

What will it take to attain your financial goals, and what steps have you taken toward attaining them?

What would motivate you to put forth your greatest effort to live a CASH ONLY lifestyle?

What would your life be like once you achieved financial freedom? Be specific in writing your thoughts.

The Keys to Managing Your Money Flow Wisely

Whether you are operating a household or a business, it is essential that you are aware of the correct ways to manage your cash flow. As long as your spending equals or exceeds your income, you will never be wealthy. The only way to become wealthy is to continually increase the gap between the amount of money that comes in and the amount that goes out. This is important given that the last thing you want to experience is financial problems. Most people think financial security comes from making more money, but most people spend any extra income they earn.

Monitor Your Cash Flow

It is impossible to make an analysis if you are not aware of your exact income and expenses. You must be aware of the balance that you have in order to be familiar with how much funds you have to save and invest. Even when you are operating a business, you could commit big mistakes if you are unaware of the cash flow coming into the business.

You Should Not Run Out of Money

This is a bit of a common sense; however, it is most likely the most basic recommendation that can be given and it is something that a number of people have the tendency to overlook. Rather simply, you have to do all that is possible to steer clear of putting yourself and your family in a financial bind, in view of the fact that if that takes place, you will possibly resort to things you do not want to do. Your initial instinct may be to access a huge amount of debt and this would only get you deeper into money woes, particularly if you do not have a practical means of repaying it in the near future.

Make Use of a Personal Finance Management Program

While you don't have to become an accountant to understand financial statements, you do need to pay attention to your money. It would be great to hire the services of a professional accountant. But you should also have your own personal finances management system as well. The majority of the accounting functions that are needed to manage your income and expenses can be achieved by utilizing a personal finance management program. This is great tools that would make it easy to manage your finances. You can research many of the programs on the internet. You do not need to be a financial expert to use these programs. Many of them have a tutorial to walk you through the process of getting set up.

Living a wealth building lifestyle means you manage your money well and make wise purchases with money. One of the big mistakes people make when they start to take responsibility and control of their finances is that they fail to assess their personal philosophical values about money. After all, your values ultimately determine how you will earn your income, how you will invest and how you circulate your money.

If what you think is what you get, then what you say is what you ask for.

MONEY AFFIRMATIONS

- My money circulates back to me.

- I always have more than enough money.

- I manage my finances wisely.

- I choose to live an abundant life.

- God is my source, I have the power to produce wealth.

- I attract only lucrative opportunities.

- As I give, I shall receive.

- I am surrounded by wealth ideas.

- All of my investments make me more money.

- I earn passive and portfolio income.

- I have changed my financial future for the better.

- I am blessed to be a blessing.

- Everyone can be wealthy, if they choose to be.

- I always look for win-win in all my financial dealings.

BIBLIOGRAPHY

All Scriptures is from the King James Version unless otherwise noted.

Francis, Hasheem, and Francis, Deborah, **Built To Prosper The Principles of Developing Your Greatest Asset; YOU** Plymouth, FL.: Loyal Leaders Publishing, 2010.

Baines, John. **The Secret Science.**: John Baines Institute, 1994

Francis, Deborah **The Joy of Healthy Living, Without Your Health You Cannot Enjoy Your Wealth**. Plymouth, FL.: The Joy of Healthy Living, LLC , 2011.

Generation Broke: Growth of Debt Among Young Americans http:// www.consolidatedcredit.org

Haanel, Charles. F. **The Master Key System**. St. Louis: Psychology Publishing, 1916

Hill, Napoleon **Think and Grow Rich**. New York, NY: Penguin, 2008.

Thompson, Leroy, Dr. **Money Cometh: To The Body of Christ**. Darrow, LA: Ever Increasing Word Ministries , 1999.

Thompson, Leroy, Dr. **I'll Never Be Broke Another Day in My Life**. Darrow, LA: Ever Increasing Word Ministries, 2001.

Wattles, Wallace. D. **The Science Of Getting Rich**. New York: Elizabeth Towne Company, 1910.

Wattles, Wallace. D. **The Science Of Being Well**. New York: Elizabeth Towne Company, 1910.

Hasheem Francis is the Chairman and CEO of Built To Prosper Companies. Hasheem Francis is an entrepreneur, investor, best-selling author, keynote speaker, recognized industry thought leader, and an expert on executive business and leadership development. With two decades of entrepreneurial and leadership experience, Hasheem Francis is a leadership consultant and advisor to CEOs, business leaders, corporate executives, and community leaders across the country.

Deborah Francis is the COO and President of Built To Prosper Companies. Deborah is an entrepreneur, best-selling author, investor, keynote speaker, recognized industry thought leader, and an expert on business development. Deborah Francis has developed curriculums and delivered training sessions on entrepreneurship, small business development, and professional development. Deborah has trained, led and mentored hundreds of people with her functional knowledge and educational background. Deborah has a Masters in Secondary Education of English.

BTP

BUILT TO PROSPER
—COMPANIES—
CREATED BY VISIONARIES AND BUILT BY LEADERS

Built To Prosper Companies
Deborah Francis & *Hasheem Francis*
Co-Founder, COO   Co-Founder, CEO
Consulting ■ Marketing ■ Training

Built To Prosper Companies is an innovative business network that provides strategic investments in a diverse portfolio of companies. As a leading provider of business consulting and training since 1999.

Built To Prosper Companies has worked with over 1500 small to mid-sized businesses.

Built To Prosper Companies, specializes in business: planning, marketing, leadership development and raising business investment capital.

Built To Prosper Companies is in business to produce value and unparalleled results for companies by delivering business solutions that support them in driving revenue growth. This is done with an uncompromising commitment toward serving our clients with the utmost in respect, integrity, and the highest standards of excellence. Our delivery model is predicated on exacting alignment with the unique aspects of each client's business strategy, organizational structure, and culture, ensuring each client engagement provides clear and actionable tactics that will drive success on an ongoing, quantifiable basis. We believe that by delivering on this promise, we will help our clients not only drive incremental revenue growth, but also bring more meaning and fulfillment to our clients, their business, and the clients they serve.

Built To Prosper Companies is headquartered in Orlando, FL, with affiliate operations in New York, NY, and Hilton Head, SC.

For more information on how we can help your business, visit: www.BTPCompanies.com

Would You Like to Hire Professional Speakers for Your Next Event? We have a team of experts who specialize in taking care of all our events and making sure we fully understand your needs as an organization. We have been producing amazing results for our clients and seminar participants for over a decade.

BUILT TO PROSPER
—SEMINARS—
INTERNATIONAL PROFESSIONAL SPEAKERS

Built To Prosper Seminars
Deborah Francis   Hasheem Francis
Co-Founders of Built To Prosper Companies Inc.
Speaker ▪ Trainer ▪ Keynote ▪ Workshop

Our mission is to empower you and your team with the same tools and strategies that have been used to help millions of people from around the world take their lives to the next level. You and your team are on your way to learning some life-changing skills that will impact every aspect of your lives.

For booking, send email to: Info@BTPCompanies.com.

Mentors help you excel to the next level. Built To Prosper Mentoring Program *(Leadership, Wealth, Business, and Health)* remains the most comprehensive program of its kind and a leader's best choice for exceeding their maximum goals.

Built To Prosper Coaching
Deborah Francis   Hasheem Francis
Co-Founders of Built To Prosper Companies Inc.
Business and Leadership Development

Our mentors specialize in giving you the latest techniques on how to become an effective leader, build a profitable business, amass wealth, and develop a healthy lifestyle. Your mentor will also instruct you on the most effective use of our proprietary materials and techniques. If you are serious about creating the life that you desire, it's time to get your own Built To Prosper Mentor.

For more information, visit: www.BTPMentoring.com.

Built To Prosper Magazine "Created By Visionaries And Built By Leaders." **Built To Prosper Magazine** emphasizes leadership and business development; it engages and addresses every aspect of an entrepreneur's life. The magazine provides a platform for entrepreneurs to express their passion for leadership, business, family, faith, finance, and health.

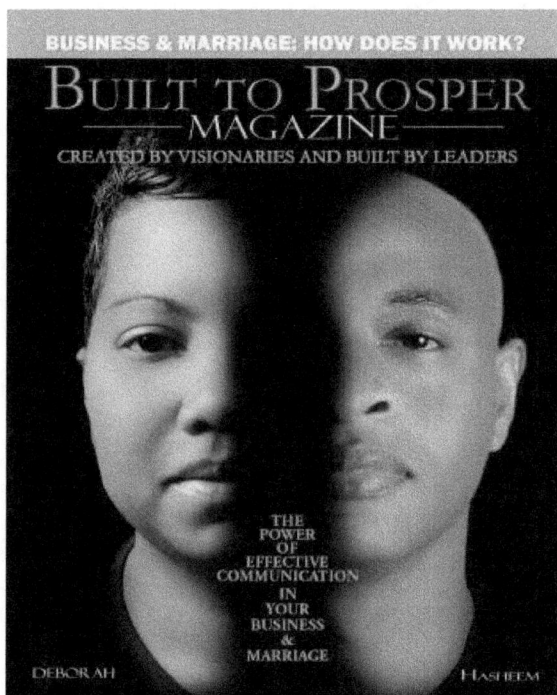

To order a copy of the fastest growing magazine, please visit: www.BuiltToProsperMagazine.com.

To advertise in Built To Prosper Magazine, send email to: info@BTPCompanies.com.